AR 6.4
1pt.

S0-AEE-020

TRANSGENERATIONAL
ADDICTION

A mother protects herself and her child by staying away from drugs during pregnancy.

THE DRUG ABUSE PREVENTION LIBRARY

TRANSGENERATIONAL ADDICTION

Jeff Biggers

THE ROSEN PUBLISHING GROUP, INC.
NEW YORK

j 362.2913
Big
1998

The people pictured in this book are only models. They in no way practice or endorse the activities illustrated. Captions serve only to explain the subjects of photographs and do not in any way imply a connection between the real-life models and the staged situations.

Published in 1998 by The Rosen Publishing Group, Inc.
29 East 21st Street, New York, NY 10010

Copyright © 1998 by The Rosen Publishing Group, Inc.

All rights reserved. No part of this book may be reproduced in any form without permission in writing from the publisher, except by a reviewer.

Library of Congress Cataloging-in-Publication Data

Biggers, Jeff.
　　Transgenerational Addiction.
　　p.　　cm. -- (The drug abuse prevention library)
　　Includes bibliographical references and index.
　　Summary: Discusses drug abuse and alcoholism, how they may be passed from one generation to the next, and the problems they can cause in families.
　　　ISBN 0-8239-2757-1
　　　1. Alcoholics—Family relationships—Juvenile literature. 2. Narcotic addicts—Family relationships—Juvenile literature. 3. Intergenerational relations—Juvenile literature. 4. Children of narcotic addicts—Juvenile literature. 5. Alcoholism—Genetic aspects—Juvenile literature. 6. Drug abuse—Genetic aspects—Juvenile literature. [1. Drug abuse. 2. Alcoholism. 3. Family problems.] I. Title. II. Series.
　　RC564.3.B54　1998
　　362.29'13—dc21　　　　　　　　　　　　　97-43052
　　　　　　　　　　　　　　　　　　　　　　　　　　　CIP
　　　　　　　　　　　　　　　　　　　　　　　　　　　AC

Manufactured in the United States of America

PRAIRIE CREEK LIBRARY DISTRICT
Dwight, Illinois

Contents

Introduction

The house on the corner has three separate stories. Jan, the mother, is in the basement looking through an old storage closet. She works fulltime, participates on a volunteer committee for school, and tries to keep her family together. It doesn't always work out the way she wants. In fact, Jan is not good at communicating with her two teenage kids, Becky and Matt. She wants to talk with them about their personal lives, but she's not sure how much she wants to discuss her own life.

It's not easy admitting mistakes, especially to your kids. But Jan is trying. She wants their relationship to be different than her relationship with her mother. They hardly ever spoke about personal things or problems. When she was in need, Jan never felt comfortable talking to her mother. Now she wants her kids to know she's open, not judgmental or old-fashioned. She wants them to know she's flexible. In fact, Becky and Matt have even seen her at parties, where other friends were smoking and drinking.

It's not just the future that concerns Jan. It's also her past, her own life growing up with an alcoholic father, that remains a mystery to her family.

Just above, on the first floor of the house, Becky talks on the phone while Matt watches television. Becky and Matt don't talk a lot, even though they know every detail of each other's lives. Matt doesn't say much. He's more of a loner, often staying most of the day in his room. He smokes a joint now and then, or maybe has a drink at a party. For the most part he tries to stay away from the party crowd. Then he'll snap, and go on a binge—even when he's alone. It's like another person sometimes takes his place. Matt would not dare tell anyone about this. He's afraid they'll say he has a problem. Worse, they might say he needs help.

Becky likes to party. In fact, she is the life of every party, and a friend to everyone. She tries hard to make everyone like her, especially the boys. It's the drug scene that bothers her now. She's getting drunk or stoned more often. It's hard to say no, especially when she's having a good time. Becky would like to tell

8 *her mother about this situation, this problem, but she's afraid of her mother's reaction. Besides, it's not like she wants to tell on her friends, or wants them to change. She just wishes everything would slow down.*

On the second floor, lying in bed with a drink in his hand, is Victor, the father. He also works fulltime, but he has trouble keeping a job. He is unable to show up on time, handle himself, and carry out his work. His drinking has gotten in the way. Everyone knows it. No one says anything. As long as the kids stay out of his way, Victor rarely plays a role in their lives. At least that's what he thinks. He doesn't realize how his presence, or lack of it, has affected Becky and Matt's lives.

The family on the corner is like many families today. Each member faces the challenge of drugs and/or alcohol every day, and it's been going on for more than one generation—passed on from parent to child like brown eyes or red hair. It's not that simple, though. Every member of the family, from the mother to the father to the children, must make daily decisions about their habits and friends and activities. They have the chance to determine their own lives. Each person is individually responsible for the choices he or she makes.

In this home, however, some of the better chances and choices have been left by the wayside. This family has paid a high price; only trouble and sadness have been allowed into their lives. That's not all. Even addiction has become a part of this family.

This book is about entire families who struggle with drugs and alcohol. We call this transgenerational addiction, or a drug dependency that is passed from one generation to the next. When a member of a family is no longer able to control his or her own decisions about drugs or alcohol, he or she has become addicted to those substances. Addiction is when a person can't stop using drugs or alcohol. There is not just one road leading to addiction, though. There are many ways to reach that dead end. But there are also many ways to get off that road and find a new direction—one towards recovery.

Drugs affect the way you think, act, and feel.

CHAPTER 1

What's Behind Addiction?

When Becky gets ready for school in the morning, she is often amazed by the fact that she looks a lot like her mom. Same nose, same smile, same way they laugh or throw back their hair. "It's incredible," Becky often says to her friends. "I think my Mom and I are so different, but we're alike in so many ways."

Jan, Becky's mom, has also noticed one other common bond between the two: Neither one cares to admit her problems, and denies when a problem gets out of hand. They both act like everything is fine—every test, every accident, every drink. No problem. No big deal. That's what it looks like from the outside. Inside is a different story. They feel like something is eating away at them. There is often a lot of pain.

This is especially true when it comes to **11**

12 | *drinking or using drugs. When Jan was young, even when she was pregnant with her first child, she never felt she had a drinking problem until she was warned by her doctor. "It's not that bad," she had told him. She even promised to stop buying alcohol at the store. That would show him and everyone else. It wasn't easy, though. She kept going back to the liquor.*

Victor, Jan's husband, is just the opposite. He's the first one to say he might drink too much. "But I could stop at any time," he says, often defensively. He says he drinks to calm down or relax after a long day at work. When he's out of work, he says he needs a drink to keep from feeling stressed about it. In the worst times, when Victor's drinking gets totally out of hand, he promises to "cut down," just to show everyone the problem's not that bad. Jan and Becky and Matt have all heard a lot of promises. But they have also seen a lot of broken ones.

Matt doesn't promise anything to anyone. He thinks his situation is completely different than the others. He doesn't smoke dope or drink every day. "I don't even need that much to be happy," he tells himself. "One joint doesn't hurt anyone," he says. More than anything, Matt thinks he has his act together. He's doing well enough in school and stays out of trouble. He listens to music and hangs out. What's so bad about that? What else does he have to do?

The family on the corner didn't just **13** stumble into their situation. Their home and personal lives were not ready-made. They have constructed their own lives, day after day, and problem after problem. Along with the home they have created around them, they have put up walls to block out certain aspects of reality. That reality may be addiction. And those walls probably serve as a way for this family to deny or refuse what's really going on.

Before we talk about addiction, let's look at drugs and alcohol. Let's look at what's really inside every drink or joint or hit or sniff. For the sake of clarity, we can divide most drugs into four different groups: depressants, hallucinogens, narcotics, and stimulants.

Depressants

These drugs include alcohol as well as drugs such as barbiturates and benzodiazepines, such as Valium. Depressants slow down the body's central nervous system. As soon as they enter the bloodstream, depressants lower blood pressure, heart, and breathing activity. Because of their effects, an overdose (taking too much of the drug) can be fatal. Years of drinking damages the body, possibly causing liver disease, heart disease, and brain damage. The withdrawal symptoms of

14 | barbiturates and benzodiazepines in particular are life threatening. Quitting these drugs without medical help can cause seizures and other medical problems that can result in coma or death.

Hallucinogens

These are some of the most common substances abused by teens today. "Hallucinogen" comes from the word "hallucinate," which means to dream or fantasize or trip. Pot, mushrooms, LSD, and PCP are all hallucinogens. Some people use hallucinogens to relax, escape, or feel happy. But it's important to see the rest of the package.

Hallucinogens increase heart rate and blood pressure and cause sleeplessness and lack of muscle coordination. Smoking marijuana, also called pot, or hash, damages your lungs. Heavy smoking can leave a person feeling exhausted, disoriented, or even paranoid. LSD and PCP set off chemical reactions that not only alter your sense of time and place, but can lead you to psychosis, which means you have completely lost touch with reality.

Narcotics

These drugs, including heroin, opium, methadone, and morphine, are painkillers.

All types of drugs pose a threat to your physical and emotional well-being.

Like depressants, these drugs slow down the central nervous system. As some of the most potent drugs, narcotics have a heavy impact on the body and mind. They are extremely addictive. At first, users feel euphoric, or happy, and drowsy. But other dangerous effects follow, such as difficulty breathing, convulsions, coma, and possibly even death. The withdrawal symptoms when you stop using a narcotic are severe. They include tremors, cramps, chills, and sweating. Narcotics are some of the easiest drugs to become addicted to because they are so strong.

Stimulants

These drugs have a misleading name.

16 | Drugs like cocaine, crack, amphetamines, even prescription drugs like benzedrine and dexedrine, increase your blood pressure and heart rate. They feel exciting, but the carnival ride eventually ends. Users feel alert and euphoric at first, but then suffer from hallucinations, convulsions, and sometimes death. Abusers become violent, anxious, and depressed. They often lose interest in food and sex. Other dangerous effects include heart attacks, strokes, and respiratory failure.

One More Thing to Think About

In this age of HIV and AIDS (acquired immunodeficiency syndrome), there is an extreme risk with some narcotics, such as heroin, for contracting the HIV virus. Heroin is often injected with a needle, and needles are commonly shared among heroin users without being properly cleaned. Small amounts of blood can be left on the needle, making it easy to transmit the disease, which is passed through blood and sexual fluids. If infected blood gets into your blood, you will become infected. HIV and AIDS have spread at incredible rates. It is estimated that 25 percent of all new infections occur in young people between the ages of thirteen and twenty.

What Is Addiction?

What are the factors behind addiction? Is there such a thing as an addictive personality? Addiction isn't a black and white issue. It develops in different ways for different people. Some develop an addiction quickly, while others develop addictions over time. Either way, it can ruin a life or a whole family.

Through regular use of drugs, such as marijuana, cocaine, heroin, or alcohol, your body builds up a resistance to that drug. With or without it, your body has to keep functioning, so it learns to set up protective devices during the drug use. The more drugs you use, or the stronger the drugs are, the more your body changes. When your body builds up such a resistance, called tolerance, it reaches a point where it can't function normally without the drug. You can't stop taking it without suffering from painful withdrawal symptoms. This is called physical addiction. Cutting back becomes extremely difficult. The body goes through withdrawal symptoms such as nausea, vomiting, chills, and delirium. Without proper treatment, withdrawal symptoms can be life threatening.

Most people who become physically

18 addicted to drugs or alcohol also experience psychological addiction. At first, some people might take drugs or alcohol for the good feeling or pleasure. Like Victor and Matt, they might drink or smoke to relax. Others might take drugs to become energetic and happy. Both groups of users choose drugs or alcohol as the way to reach their desired state of mind. Later that week, maybe even later that evening, they take another drink or hit to reach the same end—because they like it.

The more you use it, the more you feel the effect of a drug. As a result, you are willing to pay any price, whether it is time, money, friendships, or family, in order to reach your high again. You believe that you can't live without the drug, and each time you find yourself farther down the road toward addiction. Psychological addiction occurs when the drug abuser will do anything to have the drug, even if it means risking his or her life.

Denial

Another aspect of addiction is denial. It allows a person to keep using drugs or alcohol despite all the problems they cause. Listen to the ways Becky, Victor, Matt, and even Jan deny any addiction that exists in their house. They come up with excuses.

Many people think they need a drink to relax or wind down
after a stressful day.

20 They say things like:
> •"Well, maybe there is a problem, but it's not that bad." "It's not like other people. Take that guy down the block. He's in real bad shape."
> •"There are reasons that people use drugs and alcohol, such as bad nerves, bad jobs, bad days, and great parties."
> •"Even if alcohol and drugs are bad, what would we do without them? Let's not go to extremes. Let's just cut down. As long as I keep my job, what's the big deal?"
> •"Sometimes you need a little something to help you feel good about yourself. After all, life is tough."

Whatever excuse is found, the family remains the same. Drugs and alcohol are running people's lives and everyone is suffering because of it. More than that, this family is heading for a major collapse.

CHAPTER 2

Giving Birth to Addiction

Jan notices it every time she goes to the supermarket. There is usually a young pregnant woman who is smoking outside the store, or even worse, she might also have several bottles of liquor or a case of beer in her shopping cart. Jan knows that is probably only the beginning. She's been there. It may have been over twenty years ago, but the memories of her "wild years," as she calls them, creep daily into her thoughts.

No mother would knowingly harm her child. In those days, when she was a teenager, pregnant with her first child, Jan didn't know a lot. She smoked joints and drank a lot and partied with her friends. So did Victor, who was the same age. They just wanted to have fun; they didn't plan the pregnancy.

Drinking during pregnancy can cause serious damage to a baby's health.

Now, as she passes these young mothers, Jan
wants to tell them what she didn't know or
didn't learn in those years. She wants them to
know that there's a price for everything. And
the greatest price of all may be your future, as
well as the future of your child.

We live in a society where alcohol and drugs are plentiful. While their use or misuse can be dangerous for everyone, there is an especially high risk for children whose parents, or grandparents, have struggled with drug or alcohol abuse and addiction. Some teens will eventually learn about their parents' history. Others may never know. Either way, these teens must deal with the challenge of drugs and alcohol in their own personal ways.

Drugs and Pregnancy

Many children are exposed to drugs or alcohol before birth. In Jan's case, she risked alcohol exposure to her baby by continuing to drink during her pregnancy. While the overall impact of alcohol on pregnancy is still being studied, many experts believe that pregnant women can put a child's brain and physical development in serious jeopardy if they drink through pregnancy. This situation is called

24 | fetal alcohol syndrome (FAS) or fetal alcohol effect (FAE). Its impact can be devastating.

Many people drink regularly at social occasions or parties, or even by themselves. Whatever their reasons, these people are free to make their own decisions about the effect of alcohol on their bodies. When women become pregnant, another person who doesn't have a voice comes into the equation. There is another life to consider. The decisions a pregnant woman makes about her alcohol and drug use can affect the child for the rest of its life.

Birth Defects

When a pregnant woman drinks, the alcohol freely passes through the placenta, which connects the fetus and the mother. The fetus's blood-alcohol level will then be the same as the mother's. If the mother reaches a high level of blood-alcohol, the fetus will be at risk. Binge drinking (drinking large amounts in a short time) is especially risky in this situation.

The type of damage caused by a pregnant woman's drinking depends on the development of the fetus. During the first three months, alcohol might affect the fetus's bones or organs. Many children with fetal alcohol syndrome have physical

Being a parent means providing a child with lots of love and care.

problems, and fail to gain weight or fully develop. During the last six months of pregnancy, alcohol might cause brain damage. According to numerous studies, alcohol may be one of the three most common causes of mental retardation in the United States today. The possible long-term effects include heart defects, joint and limb problems, and learning disabilities. No one is quite certain what the actual risks or what the level of damage might be; what is clear, though, is that the stakes are extremely high.

Prenatal drug abuse is no different. Prenatal exposure to drugs can cause lasting damage to a fetus. Just like alcohol, drugs taken by a pregnant woman will eventually

26 find their way to the fetus's bloodstream. Some babies are born addicted to the drug used by the mother during pregnancy, and must go through withdrawal. The baby suffers from convulsions, fever, diarrhea, and vomiting. The long-term effects of exposure to drugs like cocaine, crack, and heroin can include fetal death, physical deformities, and growth and mental retardation.

Not only does the pregnant woman risk the life of the fetus, she also puts herself in jeopardy. Cocaine, for example, has a strong impact on a person's cardiovascular system, which includes the heart and blood vessels. Cocaine can cause unusually high blood pressure, which puts a person at risk for a stroke or seizure. In the last months of pregnancy, such drug use often results in a complicated delivery.

There have been many studies of the physical effects on children exposed to drugs and alcohol before birth. As you've learned, drug abuse and addiction can seriously damage a child's physical and mental development. It's not clear whether drug-exposed children (born healthy or not) are more likely to abuse drugs and alcohol themselves. There are many different genetic and environmental factors to consider.

For the most part, teens are generally

aware of the effects of substance abuse on their parents. They may not understand the extent of the problem, but they are well aware that a problem exists. It's harder to see the effects teens themselves may suffer when their parents are suffering from drug addiction. These problems don't just lurk down the street like a strange shadow waiting to attack you. They may exist in your own home. In this way, it's harder for teens to protect themselves against the dangers of addiction.

CHAPTER 3

Inheritance or Habit?

Becky came home completely stoned for the fourth night in a row. Jan was there at the door to meet her. Victor nodded from the couch, drunk as usual. According to Becky, it just happened to be a special week of parties. But Jan knew otherwise. She has seen Becky change over the year. Her moods have been erratic. Her temper can be set off at the slightest comment. Instead of her schoolwork and activities, Becky has clearly begun to plan her life around staying out late and getting high or drunk.

Jan would like to talk to Becky, to let her know that she is fully aware of what is happening, but she can't find the right moment. Becky avoids her. Victor is of little help. He says Becky is just going through a phase. He says it's part of her personality, part of her need to

be out partying with her friends—just like they
did when they were young.

Jan is also worried about Matt. She found an unsmoked joint in his pants when she was doing laundry the other night. Matt said a friend had given the joint to him. No big deal. He walked away, claiming that he had never bought any dope himself. Matt isn't just locked up in his room. He's locked up inside himself.

Jan suddenly feels alone. What's happening to our family? How did this happen? Is this all my fault?

For years, the medical and science communities have asked and debated these questions: Does alcoholism run in particular families, and not others? Do children raised in homes troubled by alcohol or drug addiction learn addiction, or do they possess some natural weakness for it? Is alcoholism passed through the genes or the environment? Are some people just born with addictive personalities?

As Jan knows, there are many reasons people turn to drugs or alcohol. Sometimes, as it was for her as a young girl, it is just a matter of wanting to "fit in" or get along with a group of friends. Almost everyone wants to feel part of a group. And almost every group must deal with the issue of drugs and alcohol.

Teens are drinking and smoking at younger ages than ever before.

Take the case of Becky. At first, she only took a hit from a joint or had a beer or two at parties. She didn't even like the high. She did it mainly to be part of the group. In the beginning, Becky wanted to impress the others, to show them that she wasn't afraid or uptight.

Matt is different. He told his mother the truth, at least partially. He only smokes or drinks when it's available. He learned it from his older brother, when he was still living in the house. He actually likes the feeling of getting high. In fact, he likes it so much that he bothers his older brother more and more, asking him to get more dope. But when his brother is broke or out of town, Matt will go a few days without

anything to drink or smoke. But now he's | *31*
getting impatient.

Becky passed the stage of impatience and convenience long ago. She doesn't really know when she crossed the line. She didn't make a conscious decision to use more drugs. She just did. Now she feels like she's living two lives. One life keeps her family and teachers happy, and in the other life, she acts like her friends in her group, which includes spending most of her time in search of the next hit. In the meantime, she's not sure whether she's coming or going, or where she fits between these two lives. Sometimes she wonders, is there something wrong with me? Am I more at risk than others?

What Is an Addictive Personality?

Elements of an addictive personality can be found in all people. It is part of a normal life to look for pleasure and find relief from pain. Some people love food, others watch movies, read books, go hiking or camping, or get pleasure from exercise. Some people just love to talk for hours. For some people, however, this aspect of their personality becomes dominant, compulsive, and obsessive. It becomes a way of living. It takes over their life in a way that cancels

32 | out everything else—as if there were only one way to be happy, or one way to deal with problems. Some experts refer to this as an addictive personality.

Do Genetics Play a Role?

Matt and Becky, as well as Jan and Victor, share certain personality traits, or ways in which they deal with day-to-day life. For example, they all tend to be open to new ideas and people, to be warm and positive, but also slightly insecure and impulsive. At the same time, each one has his or her own particular personality traits. Matt, on the one hand, is more timid, reserved, and independent than Becky, who is outgoing, curious, and tends to be a follower of others.

Did Jan and Victor inherit some of their parents' traits and then pass them on to Becky and Matt? Did Becky and Matt inherit their substance abuse problems? While they are at a higher risk of alcohol or substance abuse problems, according to most studies today, genetic factors alone do not cause severe problems. While scientists continue to conduct studies looking for specific genes that may cause certain behaviors, they believe that addiction involves a combination of different factors. This means that most children, except

those in extreme cases, are not born *33*
addicts. They are not born with a great
genetic defect. Still, they are not out of
danger. Children of substance abusers who
develop substance abuse problems of their
own do so at an earlier stage. Their problems tend to be more severe, as well.

Environmental Factors

Though this issue is not clear cut, we do
know that a lot of factors, and some
working together, account for addiction.
General social factors, such as availability,
peer pressure, stress, and hardship worsen
any situation. If your friends are doing
drugs, you may be tempted to try them. If
you are feeling upset or depressed about
life, school, or your home situation, you
might want to try drugs because you think
it will relieve the stress. Or, you may start
taking drugs because they are around and
it's something to do.

If a teen is raised in a household full of
drugs and alcohol, he or she is certainly
going to be exposed at an early age. If you
see your parents using drugs, you may
think it's not dangerous to do the same. If
you are being neglected at home because
of a drug-abusing parent, you may turn to
drugs as an escape or a way to deal with

Without strong emotional support, a teen must face tough choices about drugs on his or her own.

problems. But just because your parents *35* have struggled with drug addiction doesn't mean you are destined to have the same problems. Some teens who have seen their parents suffer from addiction decide never to use drugs or alcohol.

What Becky and Matt have inherited for sure, despite Jan's good intentions, is a house empty of emotional support and full of bad excuses and even more bad examples. Outside the house, in a world of drinking and drugs, they have little help in making their own decisions. They feel alone and may end up making the same bad decisions as their parents or grandparents made.

If you are in a similar situation, there is little for you to lean back on, especially when you feel pressure from your friends. However, even if your situation may be more risky and more difficult, you still have control over your life. You can still make the right choices about alcohol and drugs.

PRAIRIE CREEK LIBRARY DISTRICT
Dwight, Illinois

CHAPTER 4

Facing Addiction

Jan wonders what it will take to make her family wake up and deal with the house around them. A house of addiction. Will it take a major accident? Suspension from school? An encounter with the law? What about a home that is so unhappy, so full of pain, that no one even talks or laughs or gets along?

Take Victor and his dependency on alcohol. He has lost jobs in the past. And he will probably lose his job again. As long as he can find a new job, his addiction will continue. But what if he can't find a job? What will happen to his family if he has no income for months or even for a year? Is he willing to pay the price for his addiction? Maybe a better question is, who will have to pay the price with him?

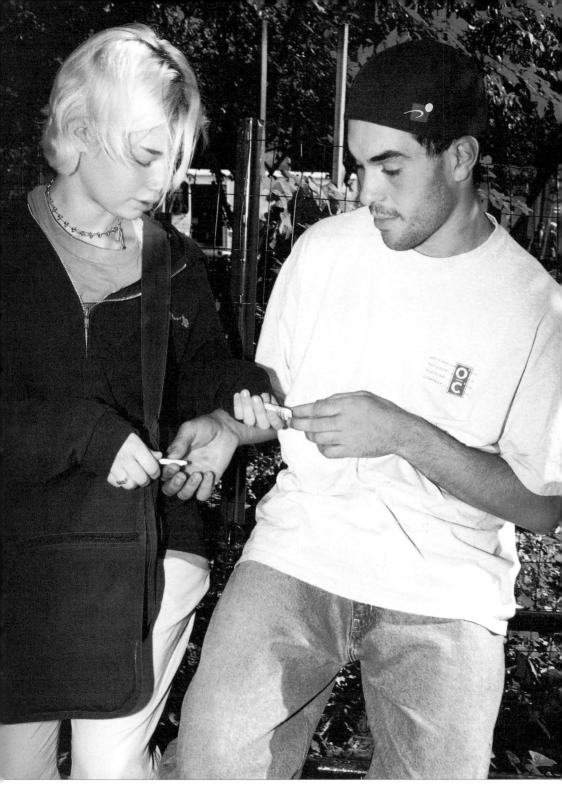

Many drug abusers turn to dealing drugs to make money to buy
more drugs.

38   Let's look at Becky. She has lost many of her childhood friends, the same friends who had grown up with her. They knew each other's thoughts, dreams, and fears; they trusted each other, even in those strange, weird moments when people say or do stupid things. Becky has left these friends behind because of her drug addiction. They have been replaced by a new set of friends, most of whom are dedicated to getting high. Will they listen to Becky during the hard times? Will they be there for her when the drugs run out?

Matt could care less about friends. He's on his own, except when it comes to finding the resources to get more dope. With only a low-paying, part-time job, Matt doesn't have enough money to buy more than a couple of joints a week. That won't cut it. He's tried borrowing from people he knows, but they have less money than he does. Then he tried slipping a few bucks out of his father's wallet, when he was out cold on the couch. But, even there, the money has dried up. Worst of all, Matt's mom caught him taking money out of her purse. There wasn't anything to say. He felt small and ashamed. What is he going to do next? Rob people in the streets or burglarize homes? Sell dope to buy his own?

Jan is waiting for the crash. She's waiting for the one defining moment that might force everyone to face their addictions. It happened to her years ago, when she was pregnant with her first child. The doctor recognized her drinking problem. He made it clear: If she drank during her pregnancy, she could seriously risk damaging the health of her baby. The realization shocked Jan. She stopped. She saved her own health in the process.

This is the bottom line: Drugs and alcohol are destroying this family. And they just might take a life in the process. The characteristics of addiction are all over the house. Without a job, without a paycheck, Victor moves farther down the road of addiction, unable to regain his self-control to find a new job. Bills are unpaid. Debts pile up. Suddenly, the house itself is in jeopardy of being lost. Becky says her family doesn't understand. She says her bad grades are a result of bad teachers and boring classes. Matt turns to sniffing glue and other solvents when he runs out of money.

When is enough going to be enough?

Confronting Addiction

This is one of the hardest tasks in the world. No one can "make you do it." No

An addict will lie and steal and hurt loved ones to support a
drug habit.

one can "talk you into it." With a life of its **41** own, addiction will continue to rule over a person's life, demanding pain, time, and money. It will continue until the destruction of another life—your life.

Jan remembers her addiction. Instead of the high and happiness, she found herself becoming ill at ease, restless, and guilty. Instead of reducing pain, each drink or drug brought on more pain. Suddenly, the tables had turned. This was one of her first realizations: Her addiction no longer brought her the pleasure that had made her use drugs in the first place. Second, she realized she had followed in her father's footsteps. In the end, Jan alone came to terms with her addiction, though with the help and support of her doctor and a few friends. She came to grips with the consequences of her actions as a drug abuser.

Now, how can she begin to help her family do the same?

This is a difficult question, especially for someone so closely connected to the family. This family, like many families, has shared in the pain and ruin of their home. Transgenerational addiction is a family affair. At the same time, there are some steps Jan might be able to take, in order to open the door of realization for the others.

Codependency

42

Codependency is often a symptom of families struggling with alcohol and drug addiction. When there is a lack of communication, family members become confused and suffer from low self-esteem, fear, and guilt. At the root of codependency are patterns that result in unhealthy behavior. Jan is being codependent towards her family. She acts as a "caretaker," doing things for her family that they could do for themselves. She often tries to rescue her family from the consequences of their behavior. But Jan can't save her family from their problems. And she's feeling angry at herself and resentful towards her family because of the things she does for them.

Jan has decided to stop covering up the mistakes of her family. From now on, they must deal with the consequences of their actions. Becky will have to explain her school absences to the principal. Victor will have to call in "sick" on his own. Matt will have to pay for his own habits. Only when Becky, Victor, and Matt realize how destructive their habits are will they be able to begin thinking about recovery.

Confronting Family Members

By joining a self-help group like Al-Anon

Communication is an essential part of any family.

44 or Nar-Anon (for family members of addicts), Jan will begin to take part in a community of support, which she hopes will eventually be a source of support for her family.

There are effective ways to confront your loved ones about drug and alcohol addiction. For instance, during a calm and sober moment, Jan will talk to Becky and Victor about their addictions and how they feel about their lives. She'll let them know about her own experience recovering from addiction and growing up in a home with alcoholism, things she has never shared with her family. She will let them know about her own mistakes, as well as the way she learned to deal with her problems. At the same time, she will let them know how their addictions are hurting the family. In very specific terms, she will bring up lost friends, lost opportunities, and debts owed. She'll be even more specific, showing the impact of their addictions on the family in the last few days.

This might be the bitter truth that none of them wants to hear. That's why it's important to talk at a time when the family members are sober and straight. At the same time, this is the beginning of the process of realization. The first step means confronting or dealing with the addictions in the family. Jan will not just stop with the problems. Through the self-help group, she will be able to offer the others a chance to talk or meet with other people at a specific time, and at a specific location. What Jan is trying to do is clear. She wants to bring Victor, Becky, and Matt back together as a family, and say good-bye to the addiction in their lives.

CHAPTER 5

Starting a New Generation

Jan, Victor, Becky, and Matt are making a big change to their home. It will not turn their home into a palace or even a mansion. It will not even enlarge their house or alter its appearance on the outside. But, it will dramatically renovate the inside. It will enhance the comfort of their home, and stabilize a foundation that has been faulty for years. In the end, this change will save their home and lives.

This family has decided to become drug-free. It was not an overnight decision. In fact, they are still in the process of building this difficult decision into their lives each day and making it a permanent part of their existence. This means they will need to make this decision every day of

Talking with peer groups who have similar problems helps teens with many issues.

their lives—in the good times and the bad times. This part of their home, their lives, will be under construction forever.

This is how it happened. Jan decided to attend a meeting of a local self-help group, which included relatives and friends of other substance abusers. It was not easy. In fact, after the first meeting, Jan didn't want to go back. It made her feel as if the burden was too much for one person. Why was she there and not the others in her family? Weren't they the ones in need of help? How could she convince them to stop?

The next week Jan convinced Matt to go to the meeting with her. He went reluctantly, acting as if he was doing his mom a favor. At the meeting, Matt heard other

48 people talk about their experiences, their dilemmas, and their struggles to help people in their own families. He heard how much pain was being caused. He heard stories about broken relationships, lost jobs, failing grades, and despair. He heard about scenes of violence and threats. He heard about black-outs, car accidents, robberies, and encounters with the police. He heard about deaths. And what he heard shocked him. Some of it sounded just like his own family. Matt looked at Jan, and without a word both had the same realization: Our family needs help. And, with the support and understanding of others, we are the ones who need to make the first steps.

Coming to Terms with Addiction

Jan and Matt were willing to make a change and make the house drug-free. And they were willing to begin the process of communication about addiction in their house.

It took Becky longer to come to terms with her addiction. It wasn't as easy for her to talk about her problems, let alone admit her addiction. Remember, her addiction had become a key element of her life, the driving force behind her daily activities. She needed more than the self-help group could provide at that moment. With the *49* support of her family, she was offered a chance to enter a special outpatient treatment program. Working with professional counselors and trained health care workers, she attended the outpatient program during the day, while staying home in the evenings. This was a critical part for Becky. She felt she needed the comfort of her home and the support of her mother and brother.

Victor was in a totally different situation. His addiction had gone on for years. He was jobless again, and sinking deeper and deeper into the grip of alcohol. He was suffering from depression. At the same time, he was reaching a serious physical situation: He was on the verge of liver and heart problems. For Victor, it was necessary to find an inpatient treatment center, where he could dedicate himself completely to his recovery. It is always difficult to face the problems of addiction, especially when they've gone on for so long. Leaving his home was difficult for Victor, but the home he left was not the home of his family or even his dreams. It was a false home of alcohol, addiction, and hopelessness.

Matt and Becky understand that they need to look for and find other passions and activities that will enrich their lives,

Being involved in other, more positive activities will help you stay drug-free.

such as music, art, books, movies, hiking, playing sports, talking and sharing with friends, even cooking. It means a new look at school, and a new perspective on what roles they can play in determining their own studies and education. They have decided to find friends who also share these ideas and dreams, and who are building a future, not an end, for their lives.

Creating a Support System

No family changes overnight, especially a family that has struggled with drug and alcohol addiction for years. You can't just pretend the past doesn't exist. There will always be a lot of baggage tagging along. But a family can, and in fact, must make the decision to begin in a new direction, to agree to a change. A family must say, either together or as individuals: "We are ready and willing to change our lives." This decision involves a commitment, a promise, or even a written contract or agreement that addiction in the family has gone too far, for too long. Now is the time to change.

Now what? All the best intentions mean nothing if people do not act on them. We all know talk, without action, is only talk. Look at Jan and her family. One of the first things they agreed on was a set of simple

52 | rules. No illegal drugs in the house. No use of prescription drugs without the consent and advice of a doctor. No alcohol in the house. No one who is drunk or stoned is allowed in the house.

These rules are firm. And rules alone, especially in this situation, do not provide a plan for the future. Therefore, Jan and her family needed to come up with some other parts of the equation. These include open communication, healthy alternatives, and a genuine support system.

Communication

It is not easy talking about drug and alcohol addiction. It is even more difficult for teens and their parents to deal with the issue. In this house, where addiction has caused a lot of pain and suffering, no one had a very good track record with communication. In fact, that was part of the problem. Jan didn't know how to talk to Becky; Becky didn't know how to explain her situation to her mom; Matt didn't want anyone to know what he was doing; Victor didn't talk to anyone. Open communication is when people make a real effort to listen to others, listen to their complaints, problems, even their excuses. It is not a time for debating or arguing or judging. It is a time to listen.

And then it is a time to share your own thoughts and ideas and concerns.

Self-Help Groups

Jan and Matt found it easier to communicate after going to their self-help meetings. Self-help groups are informal gatherings of people with similar problems, including alcohol or drug abuse and other addictions. There are many types of self-help groups, such as Alcoholics Anonymous (AA) and Narcotics Anonymous (NA), as well as some with a religious slant. Others have a family or a community approach, and many more have other particular methods and philosophies. Some groups meet once a week, while others meet every day. Either way, self-help groups are important parts of recovery. They provide people with support, experience, education, and a sense of understanding from people who are in the same situation.

Outpatient Programs

Becky felt she couldn't handle her addiction on her own. Therefore, she chose to go to an outpatient program. She went to a counseling program during the day, and then returned home during the evening. She met with professional counselors, as well as

A drug counselor can help teens through tough times during recovery.

other teens in the same situation. This type of intensive treatment is sometimes necessary for a few weeks or a month, and is followed by weekly meetings. Perhaps, at a certain point, Becky will want to join her mom and Matt at their self-help group.

Inpatient Programs

Victor realized that he couldn't handle an outpatient treatment on his own. It would have been too easy to break his promises back at home. He needed a constant monitoring of his drinking. At the same time, he had reached a level of depression that called for professional help.

Victor went into an inpatient program, which means he will live at the treatment center until he feels he is ready to come home. It might be days, weeks, or even a matter of months. At the program he will be treated for his physical dependence, which involves a process called detoxification. Detoxification means to free the body of the addictive substance. Then he will undergo therapy to deal with his psychological addiction.

Family Therapy

Victor isn't the only one who will need therapy. Since so many of the problems are family-related, it's important that Jan, Victor, Becky, and Matt have therapy sessions together to help them recover. Recovery is a long process that at times may seem impossible. Every day will be a challenge for this family. Sometimes people relapse. Relapse means a person starts abusing drugs again shortly after detoxification. When a patient suffers a relapse, it is usually because he or she does not have the proper support system. But with patience and understanding, this family can overcome the obstacles and stay on the road toward recovery.

This new home calls for a change of lifestyle that includes new ways of communication and new activities for a healthier

56 family. That might take a lot of work. It might mean each person will have to open new doors, change routines, try new activities, and make real plans for their future lives, careers, and goals. Sound difficult? At the same time, think about all of the work and investment this family had made on behalf of their addictions. Breaking free from addiction will let them reap the benefits of living fulfilling and happy lives.

This family has decided to be drug and alcohol free. They are ready to venture from their home and take on an amazing world of challenges and true pleasures.

Glossary

addictive personality Having a tendency to develop a compulsive need for a habit-forming substance.

cardiovascular system A system in the body involving the heart and blood vessels.

denial To refuse or contradict; often used as a way to avoid facing the problems of drug and alcohol addiction.

fetal alcohol syndrome (FAS) Birth defects or brain damage suffered by babies born to alcoholic mothers.

inpatient program Type of drug recovery program where a patient lives at the facility while receiving treatment.

outpatient program Type of drug recovery program where a patient visits the facility to receive treatment and support, but does not stay overnight.

physical addiction When your body

58   needs a drug to function and suffers withdrawal symptoms without it.

psychological addiction When you think you need a drug in order to function and feel normal.

self-help program Informal gathering of people with similar problems who provide support for one another.

transgenerational addiction Addiction that is passed from one generation to another through many different factors.

withdrawal Physical symptoms that go along with stopping the use of an addictive substance.

Where to Go for Help

Al-Anon/Alateen Family Groups
1600 Corporate Landing Parkway
Virginia Beach, VA 23454
(800) 356-9996
Web site: http://www.al-anon.alateen.org

Alcoholics Anonymous (AA)
P.O. Box 459
Grand Central Station
New York, NY 10163
(212) 870-3400
Web site: http://www.alcoholics-anony-
   mous.org

American Council for Drug Education
164 West 74th Street
New York, NY 10023
(212) 595-5810 ext. 7860
(800) 488-DRUGS (3784)

60 | ## Cocaine Anonymous
3740 Overland Avenue
Los Angeles, CA 90034
(310) 559-5833
Web site: http://www.ca.org

Narcotics Anonymous (NA)
World Service Office
19737 Nordhoff Place
Chatsworth, CA 91311
(818) 773-9999

National Association for Families: Addiction Research and Education
200 North Michigan Avenue
Suite 300
Chicago, IL 60601
(312) 541-1272

National Clearinghouse for Alcohol and Drug Information
P.O. Box 2345
Rockville, MD 20852
(800) 729-6686
Web site: http://www.health.org

Hot Line Numbers

The Cocaine Hot Line
(800) COCAINE (262-2463)

The National Institute on Drug Abuse | *61*
(800) 662-HELP

Teen Help
(800) 637-0701

Youth Crisis Hot Line
(800) 448-4663

For Further Reading

Ball, Jacqueline A. *Everything You Need to Know About Drug Abuse*. Rev. ed. New York: The Rosen Publishing Group, 1994.

Berger, Gilda. *Addiction*. New York: Franklin Watts, 1992.

Cohen, Susan and Daniel. *What You Can Believe About Drugs: An Honest and Unhysterical Guide for Teens*. New York: M. Evans, 1987.

Gilbert, Sara D. *Get Help: Solving the Problems in Your Life*. New York: Morrow Junior Books, 1989.

Rosenberg, Maxine B. *On the Mend: Getting Away from Drugs*. New York: Bradbury Press, 1991.

Sexias, Judith. *Drugs: What They Are and What They Do*. New York: William Morrow and Co., 1991.

Index

About the Author

Jeff Biggers works as a freelance writer and consultant for adult literacy programs, as well as creative writing and literary arts programs for at-risk youth. Mr. Biggers studied at Hunter College and Columbia University in New York City. He resides in Flagstaff, Arizona.

Photo Credits

All photos by Ira Fox.